GW00643997

POLISHING OCTOBER

For Sári and Nigel,
with very good wishes –
George, vagis
Sümöri György

London, 2008 november

POLISHING OCTOBER

New and Selected Poems

GEORGE GÖMÖRI

Translated by Clive Wilmer and George Gömöri

Shoestring  Press

All rights reserved. No part of this work covered by the copyright
hereon may be reproduced or used in any form by any means -
graphic, electronic, or mechanical, including copying, recording, taping,
or information storage and retrieval systems - without written
permission of the publisher.

Typeset and Printed by Parker and Collinson Ltd.
Nottingham NG7 2FH
(0115) 942 0140

Published by Shoestring Press
19 Devonshire Avenue, Beeston, Nottingham, NG9 1BS
(0115) 925 1827
www.shoestringpress.co.uk

First Published 2008
© Clive Wilmer and George Gömöri
The moral right of the author has been asserted.

Cover illustration:

ISBN: 978 1 904886 76 1

This book was published with support from the Translation Support Fund
(Budapest).

ACKNOWLEDGEMENTS

Some of the poems in this collection have appeared in *Cencrastus, Cyphers, Iron, The London Magazine, The Hungarian Quarterly* (formerly *The New Hungarian Quarterly*), *The Literary Review, Modern Poetry in Translation, The Rialto, Visions* and *World Literature Today,* as well as in the anthologies *The Colonnade of Teeth,* eds George Gömöri and George Szirtes (Bloodaxe, 1996), Nicholas Kolumban's *The Science of In-Between* (Budapest, 1999), in *Mother Tongues* (*Modern Poetry in Translation,* New Series, No. 17, London, 2001) and *To Topos, Poetry International, Vol.8* (Contemporary Hungarian Poets, Winter 2006). A number of poems are also included from George Gömöri's previous collection *My Manifold City* (Alba Press, 1996, 1998) and from the bilingual *Poems for Mari/Versek Marinak* (Budapest: Pont, 2006).

CONTENTS

POEMS FOR MARI

CHAGALL'S TOMB

POLISHING OCTOBER

Daily I switch languages – call them masks:
At times a mask can feel like your own skin.
At other times, the spirit has to struggle,
Saved only by the tongue it calls its own.

The mysteries of life, of the universe,
I can describe in English now, although
In my mother tongue alone I can stammer out
The words that compose the sunset, make it glow.

My Manifold City

FAKE SEMBLANCES OF ODYSSEUS

Fake semblances of Odysseus, we wander over the planet
while at home our Penelopes, formerly smiling,
have suddenly gone serious
and taken to the weaving of winding-sheets...
It's winter now, our galleys are burdened with frost,
an evil north wind wails over grey seas,
the stars, moreover, are so inhumanly abstract.

We did not stay behind with the lotus-eaters,
were not broken apart by Charybdis and Scylla,
but *are* consumed with the consciousness
that, look, the struggle is not yet over
and at home the suddenly serious Penelopes
are weaving shrouds, funereal winding-sheets.

Famous Achaeans, what was the worth of your empty chatter?
Did you make sacrifices to Poseidon
the dull-brained but mighty? Have you ever been able
to challenge him with brave deeds? Did you ever do so?
You have given us food, but otherwise there is nothing
but nimble words to lament or juggle with –
that's all you've been able to do,
famous Achaeans.

Fake semblances of Odysseus, we wander over the planet.
The sea is weaving a winding-sheet of our sighs.
The past is sunken in fog, thick fog hides Ithaca's fate.

Oxford, December 1956

5

ON A DAWN ROAD

As I set out at six in the morning on the Dumfries road from
                                          Stranraer
with the smoke-swirls of the Celtic sky above, it chanced that I
                                          passed
along by the sea which, child-like, smiled sweetly in its sleep –
and yellow bushes at the roadside were aroused with tiny noises
and even the wind awoke in a pink mood, clapping its hands –
then, suddenly, I felt the twinge of my unslept Budapest dawns,
those raw, dazed, shivering dawns, of my ripening years,
and I felt as if again I were walking on empty streets, the patter
of my footsteps answering a dry broom's crack and scratch,
the first tram of the day with a screech turned into the corner
and, tasting of blood and salt, a wind blew from the Danube...
My memories fade as gaslamps fade at daybreak,
but my faithless loyalty will last out my life –
dreaming of Budapest dawns, I walk down the Dumfries road
and know that what awaits me at the end of the road is home.

MIRACLE IN MANHATTAN

In the whole of New York what I liked best
was the tree: that tree with its dense foliage
spreading its arms up there on the roof,
green and abandoned as the everyday miracle
that is the created world.
Life round about it was choked with concrete,
a jungle of bricks entangled everything,
and by night the tree there called to mind
a lone sentry, intently watching,
who stands his ground for us. In the street's depth,
a muddled age keeps droning, teeming by,
while the tree stands fifteen storeys up
and lives, and keeps on living,
above and beyond the racing of machines.
You should live this way too, for the future's sake,
with all the beauty and courage of that tree,
shaping the light that falls on you into colours,
that the melody of life might blossom skyward.

EXPECTANT MOTHER

I am cold. All the time the foetus
has been in my womb I've felt the cold.
I see the world through glass, from under water.
He can't grasp this, the man I call
husband. He thinks he's superfluous.
I can't share my joy with him
and there are no words to express my pain.
I await the Sixth Day anxiously;
how much can happen by then, oh God!
In the dream, my doctor brings flaming roses,
he whispers in my ear that he loves me only.
We elope at night-time, our gondola sways.

RESTLESS MARCH

This is the time of waiting.
Of heavy nights, tossing and turning in bed.
Is it the hot wind tearing at taut cables
or the touch of cramped time
that makes our nerves bristle and quiver?

I can't say. The future wears
a compassionate Boddhisatva smile.
When the lava stops flowing
the village folk (fresh victims are needed all the time)
return to plant the rice.

– Hope, what an inexhaustible cornucopia
you are! what an eternal obsession!

Once the earth was quaking under my feet.
I have seen a rain of ashes, and I know:
sometimes our life is weighed in a single word.

There is a time for thanksgiving,
and a time for sacrifice.
Now each day resounds like a gong.
This is the time of waiting:

a time growing full like the moon.

LAZARUS

Lazarus lies on his deathbed,
resisting the end, unwilling to die.

He trusts in resurrection, yet he doesn't;
he longs for immortality,
but the spell of the transient still binds his limbs.

Now he recalls the green smell of marshy meadows,
the nestling warmth of women's flesh
and cool flute-notes in the evening.

Then his sigh blows out the candle's splutter,
five seals are set on his unwritten farewell letter.
He sleeps, and in a nightmare sees the Spirit
mould Adam from dust – and all that we inherit.

These are the agonies of voluntary death.
The pains the living cannot imagine.

A great stone is rolled into his tomb's mouth –
but it will not stop the miracle to come
when lo! dead Lazarus walks out on the third day,
and looks into the never-closing eyes of God.

Translated by Tony Connor

ON A HOMECOMING

As in a dream, the tangled trees
Are merging into dusk, you feel;
You're trudging down a worn-out street,
The houses pregnant with some ill.
Love, like a distant gas-lamp, keeps
Blinking on the Buda shore –
Over the Chain Bridge grinds a bus;
Twilight, a tired passenger,
Descends. And mist, mist, autumn mist
Gets woven into evening's hush.
Somewhere warm espresso bars
Wait with a hum and then a whoosh.
But suddenly a strong desire
For Montparnasse takes hold: you learn to
Know your own home here, this land yours,
And there is nowhere to return to.

MANDELSHTAM IN EXILE

Our living space, all measured out,
Our days are numbered, one and all;
Through the steppe's silver night, you hear
A wolf, haggard and starving, howl.

This is a dead, inhuman land
Whose power no god or demon wields.
The glimmer of the Arctic light
Is the far smile of crystal worlds.

The blood-stained star of destiny
Has set out on its path through space;
There are no saving miracles –
Nor can remorse now win you grace.

There's no one to deflect the track
Of the knives whistling straight for you.
Persephone, standing at your back,
Proffers her hand. Hold yours out too.

THE PERFECT HOUSE

Everything is perfect here
The floor is made of marble
The closets mahogany
The chandelier top quality artificial crystal
The morning light glistens on the tiles
of the bathroom

The blueprint is final
The place is furnished with a practical purpose
in mind
It will last a lifetime
a house
ház
Haus

The objects absorb
the tenants
The finality of the objects
make us forget
the ineptness
of the tenants

marble (sarcophagus)
panelling (mahogany)
crystal (time)
light (dissection room)

He who dwells in this house
is not helpless, irremediable
but his life is
uninhabitable

Translated by Nicholas Kolumban

LETTER FROM A DECLINING EMPIRE

Ever more frightening, ever more rapacious,
barbarian incursions are troubling
the Empire of Autumn.
And galloping on, the northerly wind
screeches through cloud-crevices, shears off
leafy crowns, tears down
beech-tree robes the colour of sealing-wax,
shedding their heavy blood,
cracking its whip at defencelessly shuddering maples –
and how the gold coins keep falling!
Down threadbare avenues, past gap-toothed palings
the raider's clattering by; he throws
a firebrand into a chestnut-tree, and whoosh!
leaves whirl and fly up into
an air-woven hoop of flame. There's no one by
to save the treasures, the infidel
can pillage unhindered, now only
the scattered watchtowers of silver fir are left standing.
And still the conquest is not complete. In vain
do frost-riders patrol down by the river,
in vain does the Khan exact ransom from the milder
October colours, from sky-blue and green;
the survivors learn how to live. Naked as
cornstalks rent and torn, and with earth's bitterness.
Once the marauders have cleared off, their savage
symbols will melt too trickling down the gardens, and then
of a sudden the new
but eternal year will rise and raise with sunshine a still
more beautiful empire.

FROM A TRAVELLER'S NOTEBOOK

In Ruritania
there are no plugs in the baths
lavatory seats aren't sat upon but vomited over
offices smell of cabbage
culture of cheap eau de Cologne
With thickly padded shoulders in a jacket cut too straight
the writer stalks about in the field of Word
he bends down picks up a piece of reality
sniffs at it and chucks it away grimacing
he makes a bouquet of dew-drenched immortelles
for his fadeless merits
he shall while he lives be exalted
In Ruritania
the job of ceremonial incense-bearer
is not for everyone
only for those whose past *and* future
are equally beyond reproach
the dispensation of incense is important
though it does not make the task of post-perfuming
any less necessary
In the shops there is a crowd
for it is rumoured that a large consignment
of word-stock has arrived
words beginning with 'x' are on sale again
and there are 'z'-s galore (or so they say)
Oooh and if plugs should appear at last
sheets of sandpaper and pastry cutters
then in Ruritania
the deluge of satisfaction would shatter everything

YOUNG WRITER IN EASTERN EUROPE

Can one who looks toward more distant things
slip free of the iron ring that is mere chance?
Everywhere are the same old booby-traps,
the same barbed-wire entanglements,
the same elusive enemy,
mine-throwers disguised by protective colouring,
and even on each horizon the same hillocks,
their colours indefinable,
with flowers that may or may not possess
a vague odour.

To live differently. One could, perhaps ... but how?
Instead of indeterminate boundaries
the mind needs a magnetic field,
instead of the odd chance, certainty
(weather conditions notwithstanding).
There is nothing to pour out with the bath water,
and how do you lie on a bed made by another?
Not much remains: black anecdotes, maxims,
occasional pieces done for the media. Taped music
wafting faintly through rooms with the curtains drawn
and love made to nameless girls.

DATA FOR A NATURAL HISTORY OF SMALL NATIONS

Small Nations
as a rule peep out of the pockets of big ones
and there they rave and wave their arms about:
'vile usurper!'
or
'dearest friend!'
at times of historic hurricanes
they fall into hoof-prints brimming with water
heavy cavalry clatters over them
they are rolled flat by caterpillar tracks
but those who survive
tattered and torn maimed and half-paralysed
go on raving and waving –
in disbelief the giants shake their heads:
'what resilience!'
'who would have believed it?'

these small nations can take quite a lot

MEMORIES OF A TRAIN JOURNEY

Beer bottles, lemonade bottles, their rhythmical clink,
bread-crusts, green pepper cores in a plastic bag;
a cheap novel - *Wyatt Earp: Hero
of the Wild West* (to be continued), dog-eared;
a rust spot left on the blue plush by a fag-end,
ashtrays Pompeian in their abundance, dead matchsticks,
reading-lamps wrenched from their sockets,
sporting chronicles, several days old, in shreds; the smell
of excrement, soot, clouds of stale sweat
that the finest fibre, the viscera of the carriage
were permeated with. Cultures of dirt.
And something that has no palpable trace, the hope-
less tossing and turning, the whining, the curses
muttered and mumbled as if in prayer, because
you've just got to live like this, like a stray dog,
just shuttled back and forth between no fixed stations.

A SITUATION

he who lives across from a watchtower
he whose window looks out onto a gaol
will not be dazzled by vain hopes
will not be seduced by sham perspectives

travelling does not tempt him either
for he knows: there is no way out –
from here a road leads into the clouds
built out of paper, stones and sweat

he comes finally into a haven
the bay and the shores of family beckon
and as he writes his memoirs and goes ga-ga
it's only his past that hums like a samovar

ISLAND IN THE MEDITERRANEAN

Nothing is impossible on this island:
Calypso might just be the name of a boat
as much as a nymph. As for the sea,
not wine-dark, it's more of a blue or green,
gentian, or several shades of amethyst.
But there is, as the tale has it in H.,
'poplar and alder and fragrant cypress'
and a monastery garden full of amphoras.
Odysseus, under a vine-trellis,
drinks wine; he does not brood on the shore.
Seven days – not years – soon pass, no, run:
an occasion for tears. By night the cave's
redolent of parsley, no irises here –
they've withered – just aloes and oleanders
and endless fields of flowering lavender.
The past grinds down the Trojan hecatomb
and only the gods can see that he'll make it home.
Not for him immortality, for he of the gods' sweet
idyll desires no part but, glad to have found love, he wave-like
mounts and again comes to rest in Calypso's arms now,
                                        the wanderer.

ABDA

In memory of Miklós Radnóti★

They made us dig. Leaden, grey,
the sky is empty of all but the beat –
exhausted, slow – of a rook's wings.
Carts over there, bored soldiers.
(How banal it is, the entire setting!)
And these aren't even Germans.
We speak the same language and yet the guard
can't understand a word I say.
The Book's prophecy and that of my own
prophetic soul are proving true.
The sponge is dipped in vinegar.
I pocket the little notebook now,
still inhaling the pasture's damp
and the brushwood smoke that wreathes the willows.
Non onmis moriar - yes I know,
but now for the last time I can say *I am*:
I shall be a flame that soars in the broad sky,
a silent body laid in the damp earth.

★Hungarian poet of Jewish origin, killed in 1944 at the age of 35, near the village of Abda in Hungary. He was buried in a mass grave; his body was identified at the exhumation in 1946 by a notebook of poems found in the pocket of his raincoat.

A PHANTASTIC TOPOGRAPHY

'A desert country near the sea'
Shakespeare

where screws and assistant caretakers
teach philosophy
there the philosophers
become night watchmen at the Zoo
where the state has reason to be afraid
of Aristotle
there objective reality has come to an end
under the sky of an addled myth
even informers scurry about in jeans
under a sky with knitted brows
raw future is the food of termite years

AT TIMES LIKE THIS

towards the end of October
when the huge chestnut spreading its branches
majestically at the gates of King's College
turns to the colour of clear honey
and the medlar decks itself out in shades of copper
and the small fig bares its branches
no longer concealing the slightness of its yield
at times like this at the turn of autumn
I hear once again the bugle-call
sounding from far away
just moments before the parade
and the most abandoned carnival in our history
began

YES, NO

An old man so it's hard for him to remember
yes he was always a law-abiding man
no it wasn't the kind of work he liked
yes but then that was his job
no he was never idle at the workplace
yes the State demanded it
no he never slapped anybody's face
yes beating was forbidden in the regulations
no later on he never gave much thought to it
yes at night they drank and played cards
no he has never felt any racial hatred
yes well what else just an average sort of person

but orders are orders are orders are ORDERS

the final sum is 250,000 (people)
but it may be more
or less

as you get older you start forgetting
nicht wahr?

....

why bother about details
once upon a time there was
once there was a little Polish village
Sobibor

AERIAL VIEW OF A DEVELOPING COUNTRY

Something that wars (in these parts
everyday events) could not achieve
is now realized: huge craters mined-out,
half-demolished hills,
constantly smouldering rubbish-tips,
scrapheaps of ancient factories,
the most modern machines rusting in silent rain,
air polluted with special care
(for each square inch each labourer
can claim as much as a pound of dust!)
and the mild water of the lake which, at best,
gives you dysentery.
This is where we stand and I haven't yet mentioned
the clouds of lead billowing from exhausts,
the theoretical sewage-works and the much-guaranteed
nuclear plants (as to their safety you may swear to it
provided the courts don't object to perjury).
Let's not wait till the next earthquake:
if nature won't do it, man is sure
to do his utmost to create a country
where life is no longer worth living.

GLOSS ON NADEZHDA*

'And what is it makes you think you should be happy?'
asked Osip of Nadezhda. They had, though,
some happy hours, some moments, but many more
were drenched in fear as gauze in thick blood.
Osip paid for poetry with his life; Nadezhda
spent hers embalming the frail body of lyric,
and uplifting it, tearfully. But as a French visitor
in '77 put it, 'What after all can one expect from this country?'
Nadezhda's hopes were modest: to go as one came –
in bed, among pillows. Not in 50 below zero,
She expected no miracles: maybe an earthquake will raise
the seemingly dead, but peonies won't grow on the steppe,
neither will gladioli sprout from cement; dulled minds
will be dulled further with vodka, and as for the young,
they almost wish for the Thrilling Thirties again,
when the butcher state, smooth-fronted and muscular,
still looked out confidently towards the future: the state
which struck all other opinions,
all private beliefs and private lives stone dead,
which boiled the plentiful bones of peasant millions
in its vast cauldron – for its wretchedly meagre soup.

*Wife of Russian poet Osip Mandelshtam and author of the memoir *Hope Against Hope*.

CHRISTMAS 1956

At this stage we suspect and yet should know
there's no way back. The papers paint a bleak
deserted city where sporadic rifles
rattle against a snow swaddled night.
Here Regent Street is one vast jeweller's
and 'Silent Night' spills tinsel on bright pavements.
We are invited, Andris and I, to Epping,
to an English family. We're greeted with
a crackling fire, roast turkey, and an ancient
pudding like a shrunken head (preserved
in brandy, edible). We dance in the vague darkness,
embrace the shapely daughters of the house
(but sleep with rubber bottles, not with them.)
Back home there are no mass arrests as yet,
the writers' union functions, but omens are bad,
not knowing (though suspecting) what may follow:
in our case Oxford, for friends who stayed behind
the well-known prisons, semi-skilled employment;
a dark low Christmas this, the last we spend
(or even partly spend) in Hungary.

Translated by George Szirtes

MY MANIFOLD CITY

My manifold city, I summon up
your image through the lenses of the seasons.
Trudging to school (in short trousers)
down an alley white with hoar-frost, when
a small bird hops over a frozen puddle:
A-B-A-B, and look, I've got a poem.
Spring: riverside kisses drowned in sighs,
buds exploding in the Museum Gardens.
Then sultry summertime, on the Island roses
surrounding me with fragrance there, and love
is unexpected fireworks on Gellért Hill.
And finally – autumn, autumn. Winged songs
arching to clear skies, flapping flags
holed in the middle, the bright hopes machine-gunned,
and the darkly gaping hollows of ruined buildings
in heavy rain that blends all into grey.

THE MAN FROM NAZARETH

Eight hundred crucified Jews
scream from the torn scrolls –
their families massacred before their eyes, cut down,
trampled on by the victor's executioners.
What, compared to Alexander Yannaios,
was Herod the Great? A bungling child-murderer.
True, his own children were among those he murdered. But
numerically speaking? And then, compared to him,
what of Antipas, King of Galilee? And during
his tepid reign, what of the gentle fool
who was hauled before P. Pilate, the one accused
of 'sorcery' and of 'aspiring to power'?
A wild dove fluttering in the fire-storm.
And on the other hand:
a small fir-cone a forest will grow from,
a cool spring, miraculous water
to quench the thirst of millions who struggle in the desert
of history. And a face so touchingly *human*
we cannot turn our eyes away from it.

FOOD FOR THE DEAD

In some parts of Europe still
it's the custom to feed the dead –
the dead man's favourite dishes
in a pot or canister or simply on a plate
are set beside the grave
It is summer 1990 Once again
a restless early summer now
and a spectacular feeding time for the dead
the erstwhile Titan of the Carpathians* eats his fill
of the young their flesh their broken bones
and then instead of a brandy he slurps at
gipsy blood and the blood of bearded protesters
he keeps coming back from the grave snarling
a black zombie hoarsely demanding: Food
more food more of it let me eat

*Ceausescu of Rumania

PRESENT FOR ANNA

who knows what is made in heaven –
though it was in the sky that my daughter was proposed to
in the crowded basket of a polychrome balloon
as it flew high over England
pleasant her green meadows and yellow fields

afterwards they drank on it in a pub
at the sign of the dove and rainbow
in the dove's beak perhaps an olive-branch
with the rainbow the pledge of golden peace

– we will love each other forever now, won't we?
it's a question you can't answer
but when the sky (as it often does) turns dark and when the gale
makes doors and windows rattle in its black fury
and when the hail pours down

remember that blessed summer day
and with it the lightness of the hot-air balloon

PORTRAIT OF A SCIENTIST

miracles still occur
in this ever more calculable world

for instance a man struck down
by a wasting disease and forced
to live in a wheelchair a man
unable to talk
(and he breathes through a valve)
a man who cannot move more
than two fingers of one hand

a brain of demonic power and two thin fingers
TALKING in a synthetic voice

the human wreck of a genius
who calculates the unimaginable
sees back to the beginning of the Cosmos
and denies the existence of God

....

as for God
(let's face it, a *singularity*)
He does not deny him
the right to deny

AUTUMN MONOLOGUE

The tart sweetness of apples nipped by frost
is what I praise now, when through the crystalline
air of this languid autumn (from time to time
tainted by smoke from bonfires of dead leaves)
I think I can hear the honking of wild fowl
and, if a light breeze makes the curtain flap,
the motorway's unbroken muted hum-
it's the tart sweetness of apples nipped by frost
I must praise now, for when the short days come
what memories of old will keep me warm?
I admit, pressed to acknowledge soil and root,
that all I've given I brought with me from home.
I can't deny the tree that bore the fruit.

The Hungarian original of this poem won the Salvatore Quasimodo Prize of
Balatonfüred (1993) and the Italian translation the Ada Negri Prize of Lodi (1995)

AT CHRISTMAS-TIME

out there the wind booms, no, grumbles,
makes the fences groan
angry grey clouds are moving east
and while in the house it's warm and quiet
yesterday's cannonade from Sarajevo
is audible
it rebounds with a muffled thud
from the cavernous walls of conscience
and who knows when the dams will burst
and the flood sweep into our living-rooms
the filthy and unendurable flood
of shame

1993

Poems for Mari

AUBADE

If I fall asleep, your head upon my shoulder,
the hectic week's harassment, in your arms,
gives way to comfort and fulfilled desire:
it is your body's quiet cool that calms.
When I wake, dearest, let it be to joy
at your eyes' light and the down over your thighs.
Would I sell my soul just for a metaphor?
Only if your kisses were the prize.

THE CONTRADICTION RESOLVED

Our habits – they're so many dragon's eggs.
Disturbed mornings, unsettled, harassed days
kindle my indignation, feeding it:
isn't it scandalous that *you're* not *me?*
And if *I'm* not *you* – how can we stand each other?
All our things are stamped with otherness.
In bed when I reach towards you and you kiss me,
we both suspend the negation left unspoken
and join like the twin shells clamped round a pearl.
(So otherness after all is worth accepting.)
Of what I am, then, be the better part.

THE ADDRESSEE OF THE POEM
For Mari

No, not for posterity: that's all dust and vanity.
It's for myself I write and for all
who live and who, living, perhaps read (my language)
and so perhaps read these lines
meant for a poem (what makes a poem a poem?)
and perhaps pause for a moment to wonder,
of the man who has written this, what kind of man he is.
And perhaps, my First Reader, you too understand
that the most important thing in all of this
is the outstretched finger that sparks on another (yours)
and that the one smile, gesture, word of encouragement
you receive this measured speech with is worth more
than anything that's 'beautiful' or 'eternal', and that the poem
is even yours when *you* are not addressed.

A GARDEN IN PROVENCE

After the scalding sand-heaps on the beach,
the statues there mottled with sun-tan oil,
their genitals (some better and some worse)
offered to public view, the hyena photographers
lurking in wait for a child's smile,
and in the end the desert emptiness –
after all that, this garden is a refuge.
It's pleasant to sit at sunset
in the shade of the tall mulberry-tree,
the scent of rosemary throwing loops about you,
a suggestion of mint now and then wafting over,
unnumbered creatures scuttling about in the grass.
The persistent cicada concert has now stopped,
just one or two spider acrobats still working
on the tightrope stretched out over the irises.
Endless ant caravans progress
up and along the wall of rough terracotta
and a bird's trilling
erupts fiom the abundant oleander.
In my hand a glass of light wine, I sit and listen:
'Are you asleep yet, little boy?'

MARI IN HOSPITAL

Again you are under the knife...
Oh my poor girl – so
every year since I have known you.
Afterwards you thirst and, recuperating, hope
that next year you'll be spared.
Stems of irises
gleam in the sharp sun;
one way or other
knives will follow you.

M'S DREAM, 1987

In my dream you were the dentist.
I lay back in the dentist's chair
waiting for you – safe as I'd only felt
on my mother's lap. But you
didn't come; I waited in vain,
while others around me came and went,
and attractive assistants enquired
shouldn't *they* be beginning the treatment.
But I was waiting for you, a sadness
already constricting my throat...

A KIND OF ODE TO ENGLAND

There over many years
I've sipped beige-coloured tea –
my old and faithful friend,
my fortress-isle: my England.

Your light, your colours too,
they're so familiar – you
make me almost at home,
though your guest only, England.

Oxford accepted me,
then Cambridge opened doors
and London brought me Mari:
my thanks to you, old England.

So bright and green your pastures,
at all your floods of flowers
I marvel through the seasons,
oh garden land, oh England!

I've toured your castle towers,
and strolled along your shores
where gulls perch on the rocks –
you, my adventure, England.

And though I am a stranger
pregnant with otherness,
the natives bear with me –
thanks to your wisdom, England.

How many more years now
will I drink milky tea?
Who knows? This modest ode
I give in gratitude.

IT'S STILL MARI
For György Petri, who also has a Mari

It's still Mari I – how do you say –
most. Which parts the different
parts of her body play – let's not
probe into that too much. I shun
naturalism of all kinds.
But her soul? Well,
that's quite another matter: it is
deep, mysterious, full.
She's a primal force and,
what's more, centripetal. Also,
the leavening in both my families:
with no family, as everyone sees, there's
no past, and no future conceivable.
So: it has to be Mari still – she is
the one who's indispensable.

FOR AN ANNIVERSARY

Two souls, two parallel lines,
that have met in words and body:
so we have been for twenty-one years now.
For twenty under the same roof. At first,
you didn't believe you could carry a child to term.
Then two arrived to keep the eldest company.
Twenty years: how quickly they have passed,
filled with problems, joys and sudden mournings.
(First our parents, then the children leave.)
Hand in hand we walk over the snow,
which crunches underfoot, just as it used to
in Buda at the top of Mandula Street –
our elongated shadows shuffling on wooden stilts, and the sun,
the winter sun, just shining, giving no warmth.
For twenty years now I have had a home, a real one,
where music's played and festive fragrance reigns.
And if, during this time, I've achieved anything,
it's mainly thanks to you – loyal, encouraging,
persevering – my dearest wife, my Mari.

THE MESSAGE OF THE 'ROSIE'

When the late Cambridge train brings me back at night
I see above the 'Rosie' the gleam of a red light –
I mean the maternity hospital whose name my mother bore
Where merrily my son, some twenty years ago,
Dropped into this world of ours – and though I've no idea
How on a birth-clinic such brightness came to glow,
I look on the light that beckons from the surrounding dark
Like an exhausted sailor glimpsing a sudden shore.
It's there to mark new life, yes; but it says what I've long known:
It was worth leaving and, now, it is more worth coming home.

ABOUT MARI, i.e. TRUTH

Mari in Japanese means 'truth'
neither I nor the other Gyuri knew this
when each of us tied the reins of his destiny
to a Mari
but however beautiful truth may seem
we can all do with a little dissembling too
with an acceptance of
the endearing or suffocating selfishness of others
(most people start out from, and go back to, themselves)
– Mari , I mutter to myself, again more
mari-ing (worrying?)
You are right
but you don't have to be *so* right
when you order your half-a-head taller sons about.
Would you agree that sometimes *I'm* right too?
You, Mari, truthful yet relative

This poem imitates the ironical manner of the poet György Petri (see note, p.69). 'Gyuri'
(line 2) is the diminutive of György (Hungarian for George). It is pronounced a little
like the English 'jury', but with a 'y' between the first two letters.

WHEN...

When the past came to be read by us
in a wholly different sense,
terror gripped us
we clung to each other
as castaways to a plank of wood,
wave upon wave dashing over us
with salt water flooding our mouths and noses
It thundered, lightning flashed across the sky
and in the storm our voices
rose above the roar
to cry in despair the last redeeming words
'My only love!'

LATE FLOWERING

By day a sad-faced flower – a pansy, say.
Once it gets dark, though,
strange, tropical: it does not close,
stays open through the night. What do I owe
this rare good fortune to: this opportunity
once more – despite my frost-flecked hair –
to study at this happy botany?

April 2005

AUTUMNAL

Variation on a Quatrain by György Petri

The past has finally turned away from us
I savour Now, it has a taste of almonds
I am a wasp here   half drowned with you
in syrup nights of love

ARION SINGS A POEM

When Arion clambering on to the slippery back
of the life-saving dolphin and clutching with both hands
the head of the (almost soulful) animal
reached the Corinthian shore,
he was overwhelmed by inspiration and thankfulness,
and from noises, clicks and words
intoned a poem, a tuneful poem: something
which hadn't been called a poem yet, and which at sunset,
as he surfaced on to a beach the waves made tingle,
he sang to the wine-dark sea.
This, the first of all poetic performances,
was heard by the whole *thalassa*.

46 GRANTCHESTER ROAD

With you twenty-four years
in the same house in good cheer,
in joy, sorrow, alarm,
in a wild thunderstorm;
with a child, then with children,
with many kindly strangers.
Also, with changing neighbours
and inherited furniture.
With what you planted there
in the well-mown back garden –
a large lilac-tree.
With windows looking out
on a field that is always green,
with books on the upstairs landing
shelved all along the wall,
with downstairs in the spacious room
at the back a crippled piano,
a statuette and pictures.
With the hollyhock I wrote
a poem about in front,
and if there was trouble between us,
you bore it as I bore it.
Twenty-four years it has been
in the house we leave today;
twenty-four years, twenty-four;
let's start counting anew.

SONATA

To Mari

In awe almost, he begins to play,
fingers barely caressing the keys.
This *moderato* is essential.
The melody takes its time to unfold.
It gathers strength, diminishes, returns, till its message
penetrates the mind
ready for the charmed vibrations
and there goes on dissolving. The artist,
meanwhile, as if in a trance,
keeps on playing without the score.
Wave upon wave of *staccato* –
by now the music is rushing towards
some unidentified target, driving, pulsating,
taking off and returning again, in immense chords, to the theme.
This, and no more, I promised at the outset,
this, and no more; we are both victorious.

A DEDICATION
To my Wife

Instead of a sonnet garland – I am no
Petrarch or Szabó *– accept this sheaf of poems,
more than one of them written when dire problems
hurtled down on us, hurting you to the soul,
I conscious that I, and I alone, unkind,
had made you lose your former peace of mind,
your patient love thus flaring into rage.
Behind us now lie months the gales have ravaged;
we wandered, beggars seeking a place to sleep,
from house to house. Perhaps this had to be
so that, forgetting pain, however deep,
at length you'd find your home again in me.

*Lörinc Szabó, twentieth-century Hungarian poet, author of the cycle
of sonnets, 'The Twenty-Sixth Year'.

Chagall's Tomb

DESCRIPTION OF THE NEW MINERVA HOTEL

It stands by a canal, its façade
battered by time. Across the street
thick letters announce: *Leidse Courant*.
At the corner, the road is up: they're mending it.
Just step inside and you will see at once
the wonder of the place. There in the hall
is merchants' plenty: carved furniture,
three-branched candlesticks, huge bouquets
of fragrant roses (it's December now),
engravings of sea-battles, a stuffed bird
perched on the wide sill (a jay? a starling?),
standard lamps with *fin de siècle* shades, the blue tiles
genuine Delft. Heavy spicy smells
mingle with those of strong, reliable cheeses.
Glasshouse heat in your room. You hear the incessant
throat-clearing of pipes with catarrh. In the lodge
an old woman with a sticky smile. Rain in the street. At night,
you wake to a chime and, through the revolving doors
of dream, come the mime-artists – in and out
they walk, straight out of Tomaszewski's show:
dancing, they perform for you once again
muitiple variations on the Fall.
Their nakedness gleams like newly fallen snow.

CONVERSATION IN JERUSALEM

What's the news? Nothing unusual.
Yesterday –Friday– three criminals
were put to death by the Romans.
Two robbers, and a batty
would-be prophet accused
of incitement against the State.
How? The usual way: you know,
crucifixion. Towards evening, yes,
a small earthquake occurred, causing
cracks in the wall of the Temple, but no
damage to people or property.
Tomorrow, by the way, the Proconsul
is giving a great dinner and
everyone who's anyone is invited.
He's bringing a chef over –so they tell me–
from Alexandria, no less! So while
nothing unusual happened this weekend,
the dinner should be *an exceptional event*.

PALM SUNDAY

A stained-glass window in King's College Chapel, Cambridge

he sits among the branches and, just now, looks down from the tree
a ginger boy in a purple coat with crimson trousers
–blessèd is He who comes in the name of the Lord!–
the Teacher sits on a donkey his robe a burgundy red
flowers are strewn and a cloak of gentian blue spread in his way
by those who in a few days will be crying out "Crucify him!"
or won't shout anything will just look away will have something else
to do
but there's hardly another scene as beautiful as this one
and gladly I'd change places with that lad perched in the tree
who sits among the branches and, just now, gazes down

CASANOVA IN WOLFENBÜTTEL

Seven days spent in hiding from the world
far from adventures troubles creditors
and women who are 'never loved enough' –
wouldn't anybody do this if he could?
This was the happiest week in my whole life
just sitting in the library and reading
The past was gone and I was quite unworried
about the future's growing doubtfulness
I plunged in the stream of letters and became
a part of it, then a bite and into bed
The next day in the library once again
my fingers caressed the soft skin of dear books
I turned the pages gently, found the place
a refuge a pleasure purely of the spirit
And that is why I Giacomo am saying
my happiest time on earth was then and there

THE ROVER'S NIGHT SONG

My car, this magnificent beast,
comes to life at the fall of night.
Its hide is caressed by a breeze,
and (fearfully) it starts to whine.
It wails like a wild animal
that lives in herds in scorching climes
and dreams about the factory
where dead matter comes alive.
In its dream the highways appear
– their length and numbers infinite –
there's no goal, it's just a ride,
no future, only present time.
My car, the wanderer of roads,
drinks its cocktail of lead-freeze booze,
not yet fearing its sad demise:
the scrap-yard as the last repose.

Translated by George and Mari Gömöri

TRANSLATING APOLLINAIRE

*An imaginary letter from Miklós Radnóti**

The great adventure's still ahead,
the final one, and then no more!
Just like a sailor, scorched by the sun,
I wait for the redeeming shore
where my boat will come home to the bay.
It's quite a different world: so mild
the climate, such a pleasant land –
colibris hum, bright songbirds sing,
a butterfly settles on my hand.
I shall meet my mother at long last,
whom I lost countless years ago:
she's young, she smiles, she embraces me
and takes me to my father. So:
the great adventure's my destiny –
will they shoot me, or cut my throat?
The deck is now washed thoroughly;
quick – or I shall miss the boat.

*During World War II. Miklós Radnóti was translating Apollinaire into Hungarian. He anticipated his own death in the war and was shot dead by a firing-squad in November 1944.

ON BRUEGHEL'S PICTURE
'THE CONVERSION OF ST PAUL'

For Michael Frayn

Among sky-fingering cliffs and parchment-coloured rocks
a strange conversion: the hero is hardly seen,
every man turns his *back* to the viewer – except for one,
an armoured horseman, who faces us, and points to the stricken
Paul...
The picture is full, otherwise, of helmeted, breastplated soldiers
with – in the foreground, yellow – the tunic of a grandee
and two huge horse arses, *en premier plan* as it were,
which could be symbolic: What these days is the value
of the countless conversions (teased out with arms and torture)? –
a return to the old faith imposed on the Low Countries
with fire and sword and the force of Spanish boots
by an obsessive King whose faithful subject –
his loyalty beyond doubt – is this same cunning artist,
Pieter Brueghel the Elder.

SEQUENCE FROM A FILM

The blond, good-looking lad leaps forward and,
trampling on bodies just bludgeoned to death,
merrily plays the Lithuanian anthem
on his accordion. Even for the Germans
this is going too far. Later, it's true,
many of the executioners are themselves
to be executed. Now, though, there's a survivor
who gapes at the camera with reptilian eyes,
his face, through the frost-mask of old age, declaring:
– For a good overcoat or a pair of boots,
sure you can kill, but from sheer curiosity too:
what it's like when it's up to me
whether one of God's creatures moves or breathes
or in my hands turns into a jerking puppet
or, if I choose, is still, exists no more.

CHAGALL'S TOMB

In a small mountain graveyard in Provence
is a plain stone slab where, beside the local dignitaries,
there is barely room for all the other dead.
At the head of the grave a rosemary-bush grows thick.
On the slab itself there are stones, heaps of pebbles
and the words: MARC CHAGALL – so many years
of life. What a rich life: Paris and further off
beginning from a tiny Russian village....
By day the sun bombards it with blazing arrows
and sometimes tropical rain beats down; by night
a pale violinist hovers over the grave
and plays a soundless melody – one that
transforms this tomb which is decked with little stones
so it resembles, now, the exile's home.

St Paul de Vence, 2001

DREAM ON THE LAST DAY OF THE YEAR

'the human race was sown as dragon's teeth'
Mihály Vörösmarty

I dreamed I was writing a poem
and in my dream the poem was writing itself
it wanted to give an answer to the very first
and the very last questions of mankind

– was creation created
did it coagulate from ancient chaos
when a mighty force of energy blasted apart
the cosmos of unformed eternity?

– why as we live and breathe and eat
do we create new torments and new lives
and virtual worlds which are other than our own
in which wearing new skins we act out old parts?

– why doesn't the Creator use his powers?
why must he inflict new Srebrenicas on us?
why can't he stand in the way of foul and hideous deaths?

– for it may be God's not evil, it may just be
that he will not take unceasing care of us
for he's given the world over
to a dramaturge of hellish resourcefulness
a malicious breaker of forms
with free will squeezed into the prompter's box

– and if the despondent poet spoke the truth
when he wrote of our dragon ancestry
there is no hope that a more beautiful future
will make us forget the crimes of our century
and we shuffle now towards the new millennium half blind
unable to see behind us or before us
but staring into a spotlight's dazzling glare

1998

A LETTER OF CYPRIAN NORWID'S FROM NEW YORK*

If it chanced that, having defied many a storm,
our sailing-ship crossed the ocean and
in sixty days I reached dry land again,
and if later the big splinter that wounded my thumb
failed to cripple me, so I could draw again –
if God has in these ways preserved me, perhaps he has
some other plan for me. In the Crimea, say,
I'd be happy to take up arms against the helots
serving the Frost Colossus, or to aid our cause elsewhere.
Please help me, You, or some other wealthy Pole,
to get back soon to that Old World of ours.
There are all kinds of things in the papers here
and you can't really tell what the truth is.
Kossuth, of course, was splendidly received,
but you've got to be defeated and a famous exile
to qualify for such treatment. As for me,
I work as an artist here, but unknown and lonely –
my windows look out on the cemetery;
above the bushes humming-birds flutter and sometimes
a heavy scent of flowers comes wafting by...
In my thoughts, though, I'm wandering in Paris
or better still in Rome, where the past's alive
and consoles – where you live not just for the present,
not only for the Market.

*Cyprian Norwid (1821-1883): Polish poet and graphic artist. From 1851 to 1853 he
lived in New York, after which he returned to Paris.

YOUNG WOMAN WITH WATER-JUG
On a drawing by Jenö Medveczky

This young woman, raising the mirror
to look at herself, the other hand holding up
her knot of hair, in her nakedness
unsuspicious, complete in her incompleteness,
now and forever fresh – with at her feet
a water-jug, the spout of which mimes
the curves of her body, the crook at the back of the knee –
this trusting glance that's absorbed into herself,
the swallow's wing of the navel, the lovely encouragement
in the round breasts and the vulva's signal flare –
this complex of forms a million times admired,
this unique composition of cells, this graceful but perishable
plaything of Time with his infinite skills:
'a belated ray from distant Eden'
breaks through from behind a leaden sky.
And it is such an unexpected gift
it makes the anxiety of passing pass.

IN MEMORIAM GYÖRGY PETRI*

you'd so often say you'd be gone forever soon
I almost believed you immortal – with
your shivering orphaned soul squeezed into
the used-up body of an Arab Gastarbeiter
permanent rebel whom neither the groin of woman
nor excess vodka could ever make forget
the original sadness of being
the indifferent circulation of organic matter
and the fact that as we live Time is already
grinding us into the bone-meal
of shared memory flavoured by hope
on which the coming generation feeds

*Hungarian poet (1943-2000), translated into English by Clive Wilmer
and George Gömöri

HENRY VIII PUTS ON HIS FOOTBALL BOOTS

In the year of Our Lord 1526
Henry, King of England, eighth of that name,
from the Royal Bootmaker orders football boots.
Football's a rough game played by young men
with a dreadfully heavy ball: a sport of the people,
not recommended after a certain age.
But in boring peacetime, in the absence of war,
they love to kick a ball about – each other too –
on English turf, even then wonderfully green.
You get hurt? Just grit your teeth! Your pecker up!
So the King puts on his boots and in light attire
runs out with his lads on to the pitch; in the mean time
the Turkish guns in ambush open fire and – not fair play –
those fleeing in heavy armour are scythed down
in boggy Mohács by the Spahi horse.

In 1536 the Turks defeated the Hungarians at the Battle of Mohács. With this decisive
victory – mainly the work of their artillery and their (Spahi) cavalry – the Turks began
their conquest of central Europe.

LOST STANZAS OF NOSTRADAMUS

In the East a static conflict is afoot:
The newly Christian King pursues his wars,
His sheep-like people following, appalled
And grieving at the fall of the Twin Towers.

Earth rumbles and the shores of Ind are drowned
Utterly by gigantic waves – few spared.
Never has life been priced so low – not when
Byzantium fell, nor when Londinium flared.

If once the Cathaian Dragon gathers strength,
The rule of the Green Back will reach its end.
All oil consumed, the fierce mechanic world,
Whirring complacently, will leave no trace.

Polishing October

WESTERPLATTE, AUTUMN 1981 ★

A huge block of stone, a man-made rock
juts out over this peninsula:
the memorial, like an exclamation mark,
points a stony finger at the sky.
We have no reason to wax sentimental.
We honour the past too late,
always too late.
'Never again war!'
– amongst all the slogans crying
into the desert this is the finest.
In the golden Polish autumn
a doleful ship blows its horn;
opposite, across the bay,
the shipyard roars and thunders.
THE WORKERS HAVE ARISEN
– they will not lie down again.

1981

★Memorial for Polish soldiers fallen in the Second World War, near Gdańsk

THE GUINEA-PIG'S DILEMMA

The guinea-pig wakes.
He feels restless. He twitches his nose and ears –
all in one piece and the wire's no longer
sticking out of his head. There's plenty of food.
And where's the technician? Gone.
And no, it can't be true, but even the cage
has been left open. The little beast gets up,
walks round, sniffs the air and is still scared.
So has it all come to an end there – at long last?
He won't be observed any more, or poked with needles?
What was the whole thing for?
And what, now, should he do with himself?
Where should he go? Whimpering, anguished,
he feels himself gripped by a fear different in *kind*.

WAITING FOR THE CLEAN SHIRT

For the English it's a biscuit with raisins in it
the raisins they call 'squashed flies'
but once this name was life itself
the hero with the splendid beard the maniac of sacred liberty
who sets sail from rocky Caprera
to anchor off the Sicilian shore
and all he needs is an Archimedean point
and all he needs is a company of redshirts
to dislodge the old world
and put together the jigsaw of an Italy fallen apart
'my shirt is dirty and so are my underpants'
that's what they'd hum in those days on farms in southern Hungary
'Kossuth will bring clean linen Türr will bring rifles'
– we've been waiting ever since for the captain of all adventures
the high-browed revolutionary who'd look tyrants in the eye
we are still waiting waiting for the clean shirt that was promised
the spotless white of liberty
long live Garibaldi

The quotations are from a Hungarian folk-song of the 1850s. The Hungarian
István Türr was one of Garibaldi's captains and took part in the invasion of Sicily.

MILL-TIME

'The mills of God grind fast'
– Sándor Márai, 23 October 1956

The mills of God grind fast
the mills of God grind slow
for who can tell
whether it's long or short
that half-life those 33 years
before justice stubbornly hoped for
something at once too little and too much
was finally done ... the flour, at any rate –
ground exceedingly fine
by the mills already mentioned –
was sprinkled over our heads in the mean time
and by the time we were able to bury our dead
our hair had imperceptibly turned to frost

POLISHING OCTOBER

Like cleaning a silver bowl years locked away,
the shine of it all tarnished now and spotted:
that's how, Revolution, I clean you.
I won't tell facts about you any longer:
in the October wind the holed-through banners fluttering,
the words flying freely, that wild ecstasy,
tanks charging along in terror, their guns firing,
graves for teenagers dug in public squares...
No, what I'll say can be grasped by anyone,
by those not there to see it or born later:
I could never before have said the word 'Hungarian'
with my head raised so high or with such certainty,
so conscious of my integrity as a human.
I'd never before had the right to be proud of my nation.
And I'm sure that when the glorious deeds of nations
and their pitiful ones are judged at the bar of posterity,
I need say no more than '56' and 'Hungary' –
and then our countless sins will be forgiven
and if anything survives of us, this will, and will forever.

1997

THE GARDEN OF EXILE

This garden is unlike all others: English,
well-tended French, or charming Japanese,
open or closed, lawn-covered, flower-rich;
this is a garden I was banished to
for opening my mouth too wide, just once,
and boldly speaking out. It isn't nearly
as depressing as some imagine, neither is it
as colourful or scented or luxurious
as the view from a grim tenement makes it seem.
There are two fruit-trees that adorn this garden:
the trees of freedom and of memory.
From either tree you must pick an equal burden,
but never should forget its history:
that while you made the garden as your own,
the two trees there belong to God alone.